RUN
THE RACE
FOR GOD

A BOOK OF MEDITATIONS

BRUNO
PETER
KENSOK

ISBN 1-4536-2930-0

Acknowledgements:

This book of meditations is dedicated to Viola, my wife of 63 years. I love you with all my heart.

Many thanks to my children Steve, Gloria, Joanie, and Debby for all of the joy you have given Mom and me. Without the four of you in our lives, life would be pretty empty. Our love for each of you is very strong and very deep.

Bruno

"Run in such a way as to get the prize!"
1 Corinthians 9:24

Note from the Editor:

These meditations are prayers and thoughts that my father (Bruno Kensok) wrote for various spiritual programs that he was involved in throughout his life. Dad worked with St. Vincent de Paul Society for over 50 years. He would almost always start a meeting with a prayer and meditation. He also used some of these reflections for his "Hour of Prayer with Mother Teresa" prayer group. The book entitled *'Imitation of Christ'* by Thomas à Kempis, and the writings of Mother Teresa are favorites of my father's. As you pray these meditations, you will recognize these influences.

My father is very close to the end of his life. He is a man who has definitely 'run the race for God'. His thoughts have always been close to our heavenly Father's thoughts. He has served God and the Church with great love and perseverance all of his life. It has been a privilege to put these meditations into a book so that others can benefit from them. They are truly inspirational words to reflect on and live by.

In Christ,

Joanie (Kensok) Milano

CONTENTS

Meditation Title	Page

A Peaceful Person

But the wisdom that comes from heaven is first of all pure; then peace-loving, considerate, submissive, full of mercy and good fruit, impartial and sincere. Peacemakers who sow in peace raise a harvest of righteousness.

James 3:17-18

I should not be concerned about those who are against me, but I should make sure that God is with me in everything I do. If I am close to God, I can be sure that God is close to me.

Sometimes it is good for others to know my faults. If I am humbled by my faults, this may help to quiet those who are angry with me.

It is the humble person whom God loves and consoles. A humble person is able to enjoy much peace in the midst of troubles and trials because their trust is in God and not the world.

If I keep peace with myself, I will be able to bring peace to others. A peaceful person brings God's clarity and vision to life, because they have daily conversations with God. Prayer is not just communication with God; it's a private audience with him. He loves each moment I spend with him. There is nothing that God cannot do for me. I only need to ask.

A Prayer for my Spouse

In this same way, husbands ought to love their wives as their own bodies. He who loves his wife loves himself.

Ephesians 5:28

Lord Jesus, please grant that my wife/husband and I may have a true and understanding love for each other. Grant that we may both have faith and trust in you. May we always mutually support each other's weaknesses and strengths. Help us to be gracious, forgiving, and cheerful toward each other. May the love that brought us together grow and mature with each passing day. Lord; move us closer to you through our love for each other.

- Author Unknown

Bruno & Vi loved square dancing, shown here in 1964.

About Suffering

*Now if we are children, then we are heirs—
heirs of God and co-heirs with Christ, if indeed
we share in his sufferings in order that we may
also share in his glory.*

Romans 8:17

Suffering can become a great grace; it can be a
small portion of sharing in the passion of our
Lord, Jesus. Its value is eternal, if I only
accept it and offer it in union with Christ's
passion; His grace will be enough for me.

The easiest way to share my gratitude for all
that God has done for me is to offer my daily
challenges and trials for the love of Christ.

My sufferings can be the purest gold in my
life. Suffering can refine me as fire purifies
and refines gold.

Suffering borne patiently will make me a saint.

Being Faithful

So then, those who suffer according to God's will should commit themselves to their faithful Creator and continue to do good.

1 Peter 4:19

I must set my heart on the things of heaven and not things here on earth, because my labor will only be for a short time here compared to my everlasting rest and peace. If I am faithful and fervent in doing good then there is no doubt that God will be faithful and generous in his reward.

Bruno was asked to carry the 2002 Olympic Torch past Gonzaga University campus.

Control

We know that anyone born of God does not continue to sin; the one who was born of God keeps him safe, and the evil one cannot harm him. We know that we are children of God, and that the whole world is under the control of the evil one. We know also that the Son of God has come and has given us understanding, so that we may know him who is true. And we are in him who is true—even in his Son Jesus Christ. He is the true God and eternal life.

1 John 5:18-20

Often I will blame God for the bad events in my life. I cry, "If God loves me, he wouldn't allow this to happen to me!" Many times I only go to God when I really need assistance, all other times I stubbornly wish to be in total control of my life instead of allowing God to help me.

Sometimes I credit good things happening in my life to my own human efforts and do not give thanks or glory to God. When things do not go well for me then I plead for help.

As long as I put up obstacles so that God cannot reach my heart, I will never know his plan for my life. I must open my heart and mind to God so that I can hear His voice.

By trying to hold on to power and control, I will lose it, because I am grasping for the wrong source of power. By surrendering my control to God I will gain His peace.

The fear of surrendering my control to God is a temptation from the enemy. This is because if I surrender control to God, the enemy will lose control over me.

Prayer: God, you control my life so that I will be filled with your goodness, your happiness, your mercy, your power and your everlasting love! Amen.

Few civilians are granted access to prisoners, but Bruno was given this privilege to lead weekly prayer meetings.

Conversion

When he came to Jerusalem, he tried to join the disciples, but they were all afraid of him, not believing that he really was a disciple. But Barnabas took him and brought him to the apostles. He told them how Saul on his journey had seen the Lord and that the Lord had spoken to him, and how in Damascus he had preached fearlessly in the name of Jesus. So Saul stayed with them and moved about freely in Jerusalem, speaking boldly in the name of the Lord.

Acts 9:19-22, 26-28

To convert is to change. There are times when I think I am being converted, but without fully desiring change in my life, I can't be converted. Conversion has to come from within me. Others can pray for my conversion, but I must personally want to be changed.

Conversion can only take place through love, honesty, and humility. If these aren't a part of my conversion, the conversion will never last.

I should not try to help convert others by prayer & words only, but by the many daily examples of loving deeds I do for others. It is also good to tell others the good things God has done for me.

My testimonies stir up faith and hope for my neighbor who may be seeking God in their life.

Sometimes it matters to a convert what church they belong to. They may feel that one church over another helps them in their walk with Jesus. In the end, it is important to remember that each of us will be given a chance to come face to face with God – to accept Him or reject Him – to be converted to Him.

Prayer: May I desire a deep conversion to Christ with all of my heart. Amen.

Bruno called many square dances for the "Spoke-an Wheelers" in 1960's.

Difference between Self and Love

Love is patient, love is kind. It does not envy, it does not boast, it is not proud. It is not rude, it is not self-seeking, it is not easily angered, it keeps no record of wrongs. Love does not delight in evil but rejoices with the truth.

1 Corinthians 13:4

If we observe the actions of Self and Love, they often move in opposite directions.

Self always looks to its advantages, but Love is not concerned with its own profit but with what may benefit others.

Self looks for honor and respect. Love is satisfied with just 'being'.

Self fears correction and contempt, where Love is willing to accept and bear with them.

Self craves ease in this life and all the good things that it can possibly attain without too much effort on its part. Love does not like to be idle and does not shy away from labor or toil or whatever it might require.

We all want to do well, but because of our weaknesses we fail to accomplish what we set out to do. We make good resolutions, but because love is lacking in us, in our weakness, we often turn back and yield to the slightest difficulty.

Self looks to the world and all its material things, and becomes sad by any losses. Love is not worried by the loss of things, nor is it grieved by any unkind words from anyone, because its treasures and joys are not worldly, so nothing is really lost.

As soon as trouble appears, self is quick to complain. Love gladly accepts whatever comes its way. Choose Love over Self.

In what Bruno describes as "an opportunity of a lifetime", he spent 3 weeks in 1994 working in Calcutta with the Sisters of Charity. Bruno shown here with Mother Teresa tape recording a message to Spokane.

Do it Anyway**!**

People are often unreasonable, illogical,
And self centered;
Forgive them anyway

If you are kind, People may accuse you
Of selfish, ulterior motives;
Be kind anyway.

If you are honest and frank,
People may cheat you;
Be honest and frank anyway.

What you spend years building, someone
Could destroy overnight;
Build anyway.

If you find serenity and happiness,
They may be jealous;
Be happy anyway

The good you do today,
People will often forget tomorrow;
Do good anyway.

Give the world the best you have,
And it may be enough.
Give the world the best you've got anyway.

You see, in the final analysis,
It is between you and God.
It was never between you and them anyway.

-Blessed Mother Teresa

Doing Something for God

For I testify that they gave as much as they were able, and even beyond their ability. Entirely on their own, they urgently pleaded with us for the privilege of sharing in this service to the saints. And they did not do as we expected, but they gave themselves first to the Lord and then to us in keeping with God's will.

2 Corinthians 8:3-5

We may have heard it said, "The service of God is not meant for me, for others, yes, but not for me." My past or my present prevents me from ever doing anything for God. I have always felt that I was meant for something good, but I haven't taken the opportunity; now it is too late. I will never be able to do anything.

It isn't true that I cannot do anything for God just because I have not done so from early on in my life. If at the present moment, no matter where I am in life, I have a desire to love God, where does that desire come from? I can't have a desire to love God unless he gives me that desire. There is no way that God would encourage me along a path that ends with a dead end. For example: I do not see the cool breeze blowing, yet I feel the movement in the air and so it is with God's grace and love.

In one moment God can transform the most impoverished heart into one full of love for him. The more I do for God, the more happiness I bring into my life and the lives of others. Treating others with kindness and love actually does make life good!

When I do something for God, I must keep in mind the pious man. Piety in action is serving God joyfully. The world looks upon piety as if in some way, it's connected with sadness. Piety is actually having fierce love and devotion for God, not sadness!

I can read pious books or say long prayers or have all the knowledge in the world, but if I do not have love and devotion for God, then I have nothing. Most of the time I find myself in too much of a hurry. I want to read God's secrets before I can spell. I don't prepare myself for the inspirations of the Holy Spirit.

God tells us: "My yoke is sweet and my burden is light, come to me and I will refresh you!" *Matthew 11:30*

Once God refreshes me, I can do anything!

Emptying Ourselves

By myself I can do nothing; I judge only as I hear, and my judgment is just, for I seek not to please myself but him who sent me.

John 5:30

The more I empty myself, the more room I give to God. The more I forget myself, the more I can think of Jesus. The more I am detached from myself, the more attached I can become to Christ. It is not how much I have to give, but how empty I am. The emptier I am, the more I can receive him into my life.

Material riches can suffocate me if they are not used in the right way. I must remain as "empty" as possible, so that God can fill me. It would be impossible to add something new into a container that is already full. God does not impose Himself on me. It is each one of us that are going to fill the world with the love God has given us.

Love, in order to be real, will cost me and will hurt me, because, in order to empty myself I need to separate my heart from my motives and unite myself to the Father's will.

God's Creation of Beauty

See! The winter is past; the rains are over and gone. Flowers appear on the earth.

Song of Solomon 2:11

God's creation is magnificent. Sometimes in our busyness we can overlook the beauty of God's creation. One of God's most beautiful creations is a flower.

I think flowers are here for two reasons. First, they give beauty to our world and second, they give us great joy! Flowers come in so many shapes and colors, they're nothing short of miraculous.

Children will often use wild flowers, with their many colors, as a gift to their mother. Just the fact that flowers grow back every year without any fanfare is truly a gift to all of us. Roses give such a variety of aromas and colors that embrace our senses with delight, that, we are taken into heaven for a moment, each time we are near them.

We use flowers and plants for many different occasions. We take them with us to honor our loved ones when we visit the cemetery. It's not uncommon for someone to bring along a bouquet of flowers when visiting the sick. Businesses, especially restaurants, have flowers year round. Flowers are at weddings and funerals. They decorate our porches and windowsills. Flowers surround us everywhere.

We can think of these as pleasant reminders of God's love for us.

We also use flowers as a means of asking forgiveness when we have hurt someone. In over 60 years of marriage, there have been numerous times I have given my wife flowers as an apology, or just to let her know that I love her. It may have been a single rose, some daisies, or a large bouquet, they carried the same message.

My wife talks to plants and flowers in her own special way. I call it 'plant language'. Years ago, when I first heard her talking to them, I thought there was someone else in the house. As crazy as it sounds, there are many people who have done this with success and she is one of those people. We have a plant that she has cared for, for 20 years and it is thriving beyond reason! I believe it is the love in her voice as she speaks to each one.

When flowers or plants bloom and then the bloom dies, we cut the dry bloom off to make room for the new one to take its place. I think this is a good time to thank God for the beauty and joy the flower gave us while it was in bloom.

Have you ever thought about how you would feel if all flowers would disappear?

Helpful Inspirations

Be strong and courageous, and do the work. Do not be afraid or discouraged, for the LORD God, my God, is with you. He will not fail you or forsake you.

1 Chronicles 28:20

Don't undermine your work by comparing yourself with others,
Because being different makes us each unique and unrepeatable.

We should not set our goals by what other people think is important.
Only you know what is best for you.

Never take for granted the things that are closest to your heart,
Hang on to them to make life more meaningful for you.

Don't let life slip away by living in the past or for the future.
If we live one day at a time we will live all the days of our life.

We should never give up if we still have something to give,
It isn't over until we stop trying.

The quickest way to find love is to give love.
The fastest way to lose love is to hold on to it.

Don't run through life so fast that you forget not only where you have been, but also where you are going.

Life is not a race, but a journey to be lived and appreciated each step of the way.

Be yourself, be your best self. Don't be afraid to be different.

Love with all your heart and soul. Believe that those you love, love you.

Forget what you have done for your friends, and remember what they have done for you.

When you are faced with a decision, make that decision as wisely as possible – then forget about it. The moment of absolute certainty never arrives.

Act as if everything depended upon you, and pray as if everything depended upon God.

- Author Unknown

The Importance of Meditation

I meditate on your precepts and consider your ways. I delight in your decrees; I will not neglect your word.
Psalm 119:15-16

Meditation is one of the most important parts of my relationship with God.

If I neglect meditation, I will not be spiritually motivated to do anything for God. When I do not meditate, which is nothing more than bringing my life to a halt for just a few minutes to think a little, pray a little and to ask the Holy Spirit for his wisdom, love, and guidance, I will never be aware of my shortcomings. I will not be prepared for the things ahead.

One reason I do not love God as I should is because I haven't spent time with him. Meditation is so important that nothing can take its place. When I meditate I can experience God's love, forgiveness and mercy. His plan for me becomes clearer.

Meditation requires a certain amount of patience. A simple and easy method of meditation is to find a spiritual book that suits me, that has a personal appeal to me. As I read, I can stop at intervals to meditate on what I have read, listening for God's voice for guidance.

Meditation goes beyond a vocal prayer to the heart of God.

Meditation brings me blessings that I would otherwise never receive. It is like a kind and good friend who spends time with me, listening, advising and encouraging me. That friend is the Holy Spirit.

Spokane's Bloomsday race was a favorite of Bruno's, even into his 70's.

Inward Peace

"I have told you these things, so that in me you may have peace. In this world you will have trouble. But take heart! I have overcome the world."

John 16:33

The attachment we have for something determines the hold it has on our heart. If our love for God is simple and true, we will not be slaves to any material thing.

It is best not to desire what we don't have, nor should we wish to possess anything that will slow our spiritual progress or effect our internal freedom in any way.

If we are constantly looking for something that is only for our own pleasure, we will never be at rest. Soon enough these 'things' pass away. The inward peace we seek from them won't come.

We must ask Jesus to strengthen us and to give us the power to empty our hearts of the extra baggage we carry. We will only find true and lasting inward peace when we begin to think as Jesus does.

Prayer: Help us Jesus to remember all things in this world are passing away, realizing that we too will pass away with them. May you bring us your everlasting peace. Amen.

It's in the Valleys that I Grow

Sometimes life seems hard to bear,
Full of sorrow, trouble and woe
It's then I have to remember
That it's in the valleys I grow.

If I always stayed on the mountaintop
And never experienced pain,
I would never appreciate God's love
And would be living in vain.

I have so much to learn
And my growth is very slow,
Sometimes I need the mountaintops,
But it's in the valleys I grow.

I do not always understand
Why things happen as they do,
But I am very sure of one thing.
My Lord will see me through.

My little valleys are nothing
When I picture Christ on the cross
He went through the valley of death
His victory was Satan's loss.

Forgive me Lord, for complaining
When I'm feeling so very low.
Just give me a gentle reminder
That it's in the valleys I grow.

Continue to strengthen me, Lord
And use my life each day
To share your love with others
And help them find their way.

Thank you for valleys, Lord
For this one thing I know
The mountaintops are glorious
But it's in the valleys I grow!

-Jane Eggleston

Love Heals

Dear friends, let us love one another, for love comes from God. Everyone who loves has been born of God and knows God.

1 John 4:7

We can heal physical diseases with medicine but the only healing for loneliness, despair and hopelessness is love.

There is a hunger for love and a hunger for God in our world. I must love my brothers and sisters, but in order to do that I must first embrace God's love for me. Once that happens, then that love can be given to others, and as long as I keep giving that love to others, God will certainly replace it with more of his love.

Love doesn't mean anything without putting it into action. I must love others without expectations. If I expect something in return, then it is conditional love. It isn't how much I do, but how much love I put into the doing and sharing with others that is important.

If I am in love with my Creator, then I will find true love, happiness, and peace. The reason love is so powerful, is that God is love.

Loving God through Loving Others

Whoever does not love does not know God, because God is love.

1 John 4:8

Keep the joy of loving God in your heart. Share it with everyone you meet, especially your family. It isn't enough for me to say, I love you God, I must also love my neighbor. As scripture says, how can I love God whom I do not see, if I do not love my neighbor whom I do see?

Charity (love) can begin today in my life. Today someone is suffering; today someone is hungry. Yesterday is gone; tomorrow has not come yet. I have today to make Jesus known to my neighbor.

If I do not love my neighbor today, they will not be fed, their suffering will continue. To have this type of love for my neighbor and family, I must start with prayer, a prayer that will draw me closer to Jesus, so that I can have a compassionate heart for my neighbor. God loves the world through us.

There are hundreds of ways to love people as God loves me.

For example: Greeting my neighbor with a cheerful hello, taking time to listen in a conversation with someone at a supermarket, giving money to a neighbor who has lost his job, driving an elderly person to church who no longer drives, bringing a meal to a neighbor who is sick, or inviting someone who is lonely to my house for dinner. The list goes on and on.

God can use me in my suffering too. If I remain close to him and am only able to receive his love and grace during my suffering, that will be enough to carry me through it. I can offer my 'nothingness' to him, and he can fill it with love. I can still love him and love those around me.

Sometimes God brings a person into my life that he wants me to take an interest in. It isn't by chance, but a plan of the Father's to use me to love this person. If I ignore his nudging, I will have missed a great opportunity to show someone God's love. If love isn't put into action on my part, it will die.

God dwells in me. I am a sinner, but he can still use me everyday. I just have to be open to him, without hindrance or obstacles, and others will be drawn to him too.

Love Is

And now these three remain: faith, hope and love. But the greatest of these is love.

1 Corinthians 13:13

Love is seeing God in all that exists.
Love is being a light to love others.
Love is giving completely, with no strings attached, with no need or expectation of reciprocation.
For love is sufficient unto love, and virtue should be it's only needed reward.
Love is putting others first.
Love is allowing others complete freedom to be themselves.
Love is accepting others as they are.
Love is sharing, filling the others cup.
Love is accepting the fact that others may hate you for doing (risking) what you know is right and proper.
Love is able to stand, knowing the truth about yourself and others.
Love is being humble.
Love is not being intolerant of self.
Love is not condemning self.
Love is not justifying self.
Love is not being possessive or jealous.
Love is not feeling superior to any other being.
Love is not sitting in judgment.
Love is not demanding more than another can freely give.

-Blessed Mother Teresa

Meditations for the Day

• There is no fear in love, because perfect love casts out fear.

• The strongest of all warriors are these two: Love and patience.

• There are two ways of spreading light – To be the candle, or the mirror that reflects it.

• Don't give your advice until you are called upon.

• Reading is to the mind, what exercise is to the body.

• Many people are living in an emotional jail without recognizing it.

• Nobody ever died of laughter.

• In the entire world, there is no one exactly like me.

• The longer I live, the more beautiful life becomes.

• So live that you wouldn't be ashamed to sell the family parrot to the town gossip.

• The hardest thing to learn in life is which bridge to burn and which bridge to cross.

• Patience is needed with everyone, but first of all with ourselves.

• To know the road ahead, ask those that are coming back.

• When we are happy, usually the people around us are happy.

• Just because things are different doesn't mean that anything has changed.

• It takes 20 years to become an overnight success.

• Talk does no good unless you can improve the silence.

Bruno performed as MC for Spokane's Kitchen Grater Band in the 1980's which performed at numerous area retirement homes.

Money

Keep your lives free from the love of money and be content with what you have.

Hebrews 13:5

If we come into a lot of money, we can easily lose touch with God. Once we have a longing for money, another longing usually follows. Our need increases as we accumulate more money. The result is endless dissatisfaction.

Money should not pre-occupy us so much that we forget we are children of God. Material things can easily suffocate us. Once we have them then we must make time to take care of them. Soon we have no time for each other or those in need. Money does buy us food, clothing and shelter. But, there are other things that money doesn't buy, such as, human contact, attention, love and compassion.

Money is useful when it spreads Christ's love. It isn't a sin to be rich. God doesn't prevent us from being rich. But we must make it our duty to help those less fortunate than ourselves.

We are not here to judge the rich. We must lend a helping hand to every person in need, whether it is with the rich or the poor. That was the example Christ left us.

Nothing to Do?

Then the man who had received the one talent came.'Master,' he said, 'I knew that you are a hard man, harvesting where you have not sown and gathering where you have not scattered seed. So I was afraid and went out and hid your talent in the ground. See, here is what belongs to you.

Matthew 25:24-25

It is very easy to commit the sin of omission, which is not fulfilling the mission that God has given us to do.

Sometimes we hear people say, "Oh, if I only had the facilities of this person, or that person, I would be so well off." "Not so!" Your holiness consists in dealing with your present circumstances. What are we going to say to God when we realize the good we might have done in the world? Everyone has his own place in the world and acts or doesn't act based on that place.

Remember the man who had only one talent and buried it. God has given each of us several talents. If we think that we have nothing to do in the world, then we could say, "That is very odd that God created me with nothing to do". We do not have to do great things, but we need to be perfectly certain that we are in the world for a purpose.

We should pray every day, so that we do not fall short of God's purpose in creating us. When we pray we do not have to go up on a mountaintop to be in the company of our Lord, because He is everywhere, in fact, he is within us, so prayer can take place anytime and anywhere. If we aren't sure how to pray we only have to speak to our Father and He will show us.

We don't need to waste a lot of time going back over our past or dwelling on something foolish that we have done or said. We can talk to God about it, express our sorrow, receive his forgiveness, and with determination, move forward in the work that he has given us to do.

Besides leading square dances, Bruno was known throughout the NW for his singing voice.

Our Creation

Therefore, if anyone is in Christ, he is a new creation; the old has gone, the new has come!

2 Corinthians 17

God created me because He loves me. He saw all of my weaknesses and defects, yet He loved me from the first moment of my existence with an infinite and personal love.

He could have just as easily created an Angel, like Michael the Archangel. But, He created me instead. Since that moment He has never stopped loving me, even when I offend Him. His love is infinite, forever offering me His love and forgiveness when I repent of wrongdoing.

When he created me, He chose a model. That model was "Himself". I am not just a photograph that resembles God, but I am the image & likeness of God's nature.

God made me for Himself, not to be His servant, but to be His child, sharing with me His infinite and eternal happiness.

God has never taken His eyes off of me since the moment of my creation, and He is ever watching over me with loving care. If I am lacking in confidence and trust, I only have to go to our Father with all of my concerns. In return he gives me His all.

Our Daily Cross

Then he called the crowd to him along with his disciples and said: "If anyone would come after me, he must deny himself and take up his cross and follow me. For whoever wants to save his life will lose it, but whoever loses his life for me and for the gospel will save it."

Mark 8:34-35

Whenever I fall from the burden of the crosses I carry, Jesus is there to pick me up, accepting me just as I am, and patiently waiting for me to dust myself off and try again. He knows that this is not the first time I have been overwhelmed by my daily crosses, nor will it be the last.

If I carry my crosses willingly, then I won't be forced to carry them unwillingly. No one has come through life without a cross. For some of us, our cross might be to become a more charitable person. For others, to live with the loss of a child.

The whole life of Christ was a cross, so how do I expect to escape difficulties in my life?

The one thing that keeps me back from my spiritual progress is the fear of the difficulty that is necessary in the struggle. I must try, with God's grace, to over come the difficulties that come my way.

I must continue to grow spiritually, keeping God as the center of my source. He is the source that I can draw from at all times and not just when I feel that I cannot make it on my own.

If I can learn to accept life's crosses, than perhaps other people will see God's glory living within me. In turn, they too may embrace their crosses and be drawn closer to our heavenly Father.

Bruno called square dances throughout the Northwest in the 1960's.

Prayer and Fasting

While they were worshiping the Lord and fasting, the Holy Spirit said, "Set apart for me Barnabas and Saul for the work to which I have called them." So after they had fasted and prayed, they placed their hands on them and sent them off.

Acts 13:2-3

We need to take time to pray,
We need to pray when we can,
We need to pray how we can.

-Blessed Mother Teresa

To hear God's voice, I must start every day with a prayer and end every day with a prayer. Prayer helps me let go of my worries and allows God to give me his wisdom and peace.

When we do not pray we are defenseless and vulnerable. We become sitting ducks for Satan. The more I pray, the more I learn about who God is.

Prayer is meeting our Lord; it is nothing more than a dialogue with God. I should pray whenever I can.

If I worry about too many things, this can be an obstacle to prayer. In other words, I cannot worry and pray at the same time. They are the opposite of each other. Worry distracts me from my relationship with God.

Prayer cannot be learned by techniques but only by praying. When I do not pray I am fighting without the armor of God. Prayer is the breath of the soul.

Fasting is the prayer of the body. Fasting doesn't necessarily mean fasting from food. Fasting could mean turning off my favorite TV show a few days a week, or giving up one meal on a particular day. It may be I am a coffee drinker. I could skip coffee one or two mornings a week. Each time I do these things, I could offer them as a prayer for someone I know who is struggling with sin or for someone who is sick, or someone who needs a job. The list is endless. It helps me to give my worries to the Lord in a practical way.

Fasting helps me to experience how it feels to be hungry. It also opens my heart to God.

Prayers when Visiting Someone in Need

For I was hungry and you gave me something to eat, I was thirsty and you gave me something to drink, I was a stranger and you invited me in, I needed clothes and you clothed me, I was sick and you looked after me, I was in prison and you came to visit me.

Matthew 25:35-36

We will have found Jesus when we are concerned with other people's suffering and not just our own. Here are some helpful prayers we can pray before we visit with those in need.

Lord, take me where you want me to go.
May I meet whom you want me to meet?
Tell me what you want me to say, and
Keep me out of the way.

Lord; show me your presence in those I meet today. Show me how to serve the least among us, the outcasts and the needy. I know I don't have much to offer, but I will give you my all. Guide me to be what you want me to be. Amen.

Lord; help me to remember that the power of my example is greater than the power of what I say. To the one who is lonely, may I be a friend. To those with heavy burdens, help me to meet their needs. Amen.

Lord, through your grace, may I be stronger and more loving as a result of what we did yesterday. Lord, I do not want fame or fortune. My prayer is that you will use me to glorify your name. Amen.

Everyday brings me a new opportunity to be of use to someone. Guide me, Lord Jesus, and lead me in what I say and do. May my words and actions be a witness that you are living in me.

Bruno worked with the Spokane Park Department for many years to MC functions that often included area special needs youth.

Rest in Christ

"I am the vine; you are the branches. If a man remains (rests, abides) in me and I in him, he will bear much fruit; apart from me you can do nothing."

John 15:5

God is always in my midst. My soul must remain near Him to know that the kingdom of God within me.

The kingdom of God is peaceful and joyful. This peace and joy comes when I focus my efforts towards heaven rather than the material things of the earth. If I make room for the Lord in my life, he will certainly reveal himself to me in great and wonderful ways.

If I have Christ, I am rich indeed, for only He can fulfill all of my needs.

The possessions of the earth are temporary. Therefore, my thoughts and prayers should be directed to God as often as possible. He completes me.

Pride versus Humility

When pride comes, then comes disgrace, but with humility comes wisdom.

Proverbs 11:2

Pride is always lurking somewhere near me. It can be very damaging to my character if I let it.

There are many ways that pride can affect my personality without even noticing it. For example: Being 'overly' proud of the clothes I wear, Looking down on people who don't speak or think as intellectually as I do, or never tiring of talking about the good I have done. On the opposite side, if I fail in anything, then I am miserable because I worry about the bad opinion people will have of me.

A proud person thinks everything they do is well done and their opinion is always better than that of others. A humble person, if asked their opinion, will give it and then let others speak, whether their opinion is right or wrong, they don't have a need to explain further.

When pride creeps into my life the best way I can be rid of it is to draw close to the Father through prayer and meditation, asking him for the grace to be humble.

"Humility is the mother of many virtues. From it (humility) springs obedience, holy fear, reverence, patience, modesty, mildness, and peace. Whoever is humble…fears to offend any, maintains peace with all, shows himself affable to all, is submissive to all, does not offend or displease any, and does not feel the insults which may be inflicted upon him. He lives happy and contented, and in great peace"

-St. Thomas of Villanova

Bruno was never shy about leading a group or sharing with others what was in his heart!

Silence

Be still and know that I am God.

One of the most important things in my spirituality is silence. To be silent in God's presence it is important that I quiet my interior thoughts and remove any distractions from my surroundings. I need to become accustomed to a 'stillness of the soul'.

Silence gives me a new outlook on everything. Jesus is waiting for me in silence and in that silence he will speak to me. Interior silence is sometimes very difficult, but it is certainly worth making the effort. In silence I will find new energy and true unity with Christ.

God is a friend of silence. I cannot always hear God in noise or in excitement. If I notice how the trees, the flowers and the grass grow in deep silence, I can also see how the stars, the moon and the sun move in silence.

The more I receive in my silent prayer, the more I can give in my active life. The main thing is not so much what I say, but what God says to me and what he says through me.

I need silence. Silence came before creation. If I have true interior silence then certainly it will help my exterior silence. God wants to use me. For that to happen I must quiet myself before him everyday. When my heart is silent God speaks to me.

In silence I can truly rest in God's love.

Bruno and Viola live in Spokane, WA. They have been married for 63 years. This portrait was taken for their 50th Wedding Anniversary.

Solitude and Silence

This is what the Sovereign Lord, the Holy One of Israel, says: "In repentance and rest is your salvation, in quietness and trust is your strength."

Isaiah 30:15

It is best to only read things that move me to faith and repentance rather than those things that distract me from God.

Sometimes it is good to withdraw from unnecessary talk or listening to the latest gossip. Instead, I could use my time praying a meditation or reading about the life of a saint, or an honorable man or woman.

It is better to remain silent than to say too much when I speak.

In silence and stillness I can advance my spiritual life. The more I withdraw from the public, the more our Lord will draw near to me.

If the world could pass before my eyes, what would it be, but an empty vision?

I must set my heart on Christ, not the desires here on earth. This will give me the peace of mind that I am seeking.

Temptations

Watch and pray so that you will not fall into temptation. The spirit is willing, but the body is weak.

Matthew 26:41

Temptations will always be a part of my life as long as I am alive on earth. No one is so perfect that they can completely avoid temptation.

Even though temptations might be troublesome and sometimes severe, they are often useful to me. I can be humbled and purified by them. The saints all passed through many temptations and trials which, in the long run, drew them closer to God.

There is no place so holy or secret that a temptation won't find me. When one passes, another appears.

Sometimes I try to escape a temptation, only to fall more deeply into sin. My own reckless ways can intensify them. I cannot conquer temptation by simply avoiding it, but by turning away from a temptation with patience and humility, and turning toward God for his grace. The best way to conquer temptation is to cling to Christ.

The Cost of Peace

Let the peace of Christ rule in your hearts, since as members of one body you were called to peace.

Colossians 3:15

The only way I can be at peace is to rest in our Lord Jesus. As I live out my life, I spend much of my time searching for happiness and peace, but so much of the time I am looking in the wrong places.

Many people have belonged to Christian organizations, hoping to find the peace and tranquility they long for, only to learn that they needed to turn to Christ for that peace.

God said, 'I am one with you, you are one with me, we are one with each other'. This being the case, I must come to the realization that God lives within me. To acquire the peace I yearn for, all I have to do is open my very self to God, who patiently waits for me to decide.

It is beyond comprehension how God, so perfect, so loving, so powerful, has given me a choice to either reject or accept him, even though I am his creation.

I can accept God and say "Yes God, I need you, I cannot make it by myself." Or, I can say "No God, I do not need you now, but maybe later on when I run into a problem. So, don't go away, because you never know when I might need you."

It can take a lifetime to realize what a "yes" to God can bring.

As I come before Jesus each day, I can ask him for his peace. I can ask him to forgive me for my failings. He knows that this is not the first time, nor will it be the last. He accepts me where I am. I need him as my savior every day.

God's peace is kept alive in me through daily prayer and meditation. When I turn to Him daily, I can daily be set free to know, love, and serve him.

Never afraid to try new things, Bruno shown here (middle) acting in the local production of "Rise and Shine".

Today when I Awoke

Today when I awoke, I suddenly realized that this is the best day of my life, ever! There were times when I wondered if I would make it to today; but I did.

Today I'm going to celebrate what an unbelievable life I have had so far, the accomplishments, the many blessings, and, yes, even the hardships because they have served to make me stronger.

Today I will share my excitement for life with other people; I will make someone smile. I'll go out of my way to perform an unexpected act of kindness for someone I don't even know.

Today I'll give a sincere compliment to someone who seems down. I'll tell a child how special he or she is.

Today is the day I quit worrying about what I don't have and start being grateful for all the wonderful things that I do have.

As the day ends and I lay my head down on the pillow, I will thank the good Lord for the best day of my life. I will sleep the sleep of a contented child, excited with expectation because I know tomorrow is going to be the best day of my life, ever.

- Author unknown

We are God's Instrument

If a man cleanses himself from despicable purposes he will be an instrument for noble purposes, made holy, useful to the Master and prepared to do any good work.

2 Timothy 2:21

God acts in me. He works through me. He inspires and directs me. But, sometimes I don't follow His directions. There are times when I think I can do it all without God. But really, without God to intervene in my life and to give me direction there is a good chance that I will be lost.

I was created to love and be loved, and to be of service to others. If I put myself under the influence of God, then He will not only help me to think wisely, He will also help me to 'be His instrument' for others. If I give Him my eyes, He will help me to see as he does. If I give him my mind he will help me to think as he doe s. There is no limit to what God can do through me.

God loves me. As miserable and as weak and shameful as I am, God loves me infinitely. Alleluia!

We are God's People

This service that you perform is not only supplying the needs of God's people but is also overflowing in many expressions of thanks to God. Because of the service by which you have proved yourselves, men will praise God for the obedience that accompanies your confession of the gospel of Christ, and for your generosity in sharing with them and with everyone else

2 Corinthians 9:12-13

We are God's people. In the eyes of God, I am very important. Since I possess the Holy Spirit in me that especially makes me one with my brothers and sisters in Christ, despite any of our differences.

Because God accepts me as I am, he waits patiently for me to decide to turn to him and to ask for his strength, his help, his guidance, his love, and his forgiveness. He loves me right now with all of my faults, mistakes, goodness and beauty. I am His gift for others. I must share that gift (Christ) so that all men and women are drawn to him.

I must not be afraid or ashamed to serve others for Jesus, or to appear poor in this world. A poor man or woman can be happy, but no happy man or woman is poor.

When We Lose Ourselves to Find the Creator

God said to Solomon, "Since this is your heart's desire and you have not asked for wealth, riches or honor, nor for the death of your enemies, and since you have not asked for a long life but for wisdom and knowledge to govern my people over whom I have made you king, therefore wisdom and knowledge will be given you."

2 Chronicles 1:10-12

What a blessing it would be to arrive at a state in life where it would be beyond the power of anyone to stand in the way of my spiritual progress.

The less desire I have for this world the more my freedom increases. In order to do this I must elevate my thoughts to my Creator. This is one way to detach myself from the temptations of the world.

There is a big difference between the wisdom of a devout soul and the knowledge of a studious scholar. The wisdom of God is much nobler than what is acquired by human study, though it helps me in my spiritual life. Wisdom starts with humility. If I study the book of Proverbs I can discover much about wisdom.

Too often I depend much on outward signs and material things than on practicing little self-sacrifices. It's so easy to become involved in external actions of every day life, even after a short period of meditation or prayer. God sees the inward intentions of my heart.

Very often I abandon true heavenly wisdom for worldly wisdom. Worldly wisdom seeks to praise the world itself. Heavenly wisdom goes against my nature because it values humility and the 'fear of the Lord', not the power of the world I live in.

Prayer: May God enlighten me with His wisdom so that I may live daily in his creation.

Who is my Neighbor?

One of the teachers of the law came and heard them debating. Noticing that Jesus had given them a good answer, he asked him, "Of all the commandments, which is the most important?"

"The most important one", answered Jesus, "is this: 'Hear, O Israel, the Lord our God, the Lord is one. Love the Lord your God with all your heart and with all your soul and with all your mind and with all your strength.' The second is this: 'Love your neighbor as yourself.' There is no commandment greater than these."

Mark 12: 28-34

Who is my neighbor? Someone who is materially or spiritually poor, someone hungry for food or love; someone who needs clothing, or maybe someone with a lack of the knowledge of God's love for them. They can be searching for shelter or for a place where there is love and compassion.

If we are in a position to help our neighbor in any way, besides material things, then it is up to us to let them know about God, about His kindness, His forgiveness, and His endless love for each one of us.

Today and everyday, Jesus comes among his people. He comes in the hurt bodies of the poor. He even comes in the rich who are surrounded by many riches.

He comes in the loneliness of the hearts of His people. Often, we let Him pass without noticing Him.

In the service of the poor an opportunity is offered to us to do something wonderful for the honor and glory of God. It makes no difference who it is; we should try to treat our neighbor as we would treat Jesus, Himself.

It is easy to show our love to those who are far away, maybe through an email, a phone call, or a letter. It's not always easy to love those who are right next door to us. It is much easier to give them some food to satisfy their hunger rather than respond to the loneliness and suffering of someone; this is true even in our own family.

Christ is present today in the people who are considered unwanted, who have no job, who do not receive any attention or care, who are hungry, who need clothing or shelter. Our government or society will probably give them some food or other material things. It is up to us as Christians, to speak to the lonely and to those who do not experience love.

How can I love my neighbor today? Who is my neighbor?

Words to Live by

"At the end of life, we will not be judged by how many diplomas we have received, how much money we have made, how many great things we have done. We will be judged by this – 'I was hungry and you gave me to eat. I was naked and you clothed me. I was homeless and you took me in.' Hungry not only for bread, but hungry for love. Naked not only for clothing, but naked of human dignity and respect. Homeless not only for want of a room of bricks, but homeless because of rejection. This is Christ's distressing disguise."

-Blessed Mother Teresa

If we really want to love, we must learn how to forgive.

I would rather make mistakes in kindness and compassion than to work miracles in unkindness and hardness.

There is no limit to love, because God is love and love is God and His love is infinite.

Because we cannot see Christ, we cannot express our love to him, but our neighbor we can always see.

Love is a fruit that is in season at all times and within reach of everyone.

-Blessed Mother Teresa

ABOUT THE AUTHOR

Bruno Kensok lives in Spokane, WA with his wife Viola, of 63 years. They have 4 children, 14 grandchildren, and 12 great grandchildren. Bruno and 'Vi' have spent most of their lives serving the homeless, the sick, the imprisoned and the severely handicapped.

Bruno participated in Spokane's annual Bloomsday race for many years, even well into his 70's. In 2002 he carried the Olympic Torch as it traveled through Spokane en route to the Winter Olympics in Salt Lake City.

It was always his heart's desire to work in Calcutta, and to be able to meet Mother Teresa. His dream came true in 1994, when he traveled to India where he worked with the Sisters of Charity for three weeks, gleaning information about how to serve the poor better in Spokane. While there, he was able to meet privately with Mother Teresa on three occasions.

Bruno's work with the St Vincent De Paul Society in Spokane spans over 50 years. His work there included home visits, building food baskets, delivering furniture, recruiting new members, and serving as a council president. Many friends and acquaintances have been touched by Bruno's enthusiasm for God. He has always found a way to share about his faith with great humor and great love.

NOTES

NOTES

Made in the USA
Las Vegas, NV
13 February 2023